Painting My Thoughts

Painting
My
Thoughts

A collection of poems

Jose Chacon

To those who can't find the words for themselves,
borrow mine

Published by Chacon & Co. Press
ISBN: 979-8-9937950-0-3
Cover design by Jose Chacon
Printed in the United States of America
First Edition

For permissions or inquiries, please reach out via Instagram:
@josechaconauthor

Acknowledgments

I'm grateful to everyone who saw my potential and encouraged me to express myself through writing. I couldn't have done this without your support. To the poets whose beautiful work inspired me—thank you for showing me what language can do. I'm especially grateful to my family: you made me feel like I was the best in the world. And to the readers: thank you for your time, your attention, and your willingness to listen.

Contents

Letter to the Reader

Dear Reader,

Poetry has played an important part in my life. In a way, it is my life. It is the venue to which I turned when I needed to express how I felt, but I didn't know how. It saved my life. I was able to take something personal and transform it into something beautiful for myself.

This book shares moments from my life that I wanted to capture. I wanted to share what I felt in hopes that it might help someone else. There's silliness here, and moments of grief, too. I want to share a laugh and let out some tears.

I use various poetic styles to capture my moment. I began only knowing the free verse form, but I discovered new forms. I enjoyed the challenge of learning how to write the various poetry forms out of the hundreds that exist. I include the ones I used in the appendix.

I share pieces of myself with the wish that pieces of you awaken as mine have while working on this book. Thank you for your time.

Sincerely,

Jose Chacon

Wonder

The Blooming Tulip

I outgrew my favorite pot to bloom,
Soil so soft, comfortable to rest.

Comfortable to rest, budding in youth,
Waiting for water, air and food.

How can I grow, waiting for water,
When my roots need stretching and space,

My roots need stretching, transplanting anew,
I can't remain, while some buds refuse.

A tulip must open, I can't remain,
Late spring is calling, sorrowful shift.

A sorrowful shift, you blame the sun,
This pot held all my delight, I'm flowering.

Flowering in all my delight, I'm glad,
I outgrew my favorite pot to bloom.

Why Write?

I saw a broken heart, so I decided to write.
I saw the loneliness, I picked up a pen.
I heard the cries, I wondered "why?"
I felt lost, so the stories began.
People need some help, maybe me.
Clearly I think, when I slowly breathe.
Lines on mirrors, I see beneath.
Reflecting, obscuring, falling leaves.
I saw the broken heart, healing me.

Capturing the Moment

Capturing the moment
As letters in a bottle,   Formed onto canvas,
                                                 With solid foundations,
Words define the unseen   As opaque lines form.
            Gentle strokes, light edits,
Alliteration and metaphors,   Layering, polymerizing,
                                            As air takes the water to play,
        Becoming defined, understood.
Selecting and picking,   Flowers, cicadas, things I touch,
Venturing through,   Fluorescent winter blues,
Given enough energy,   UV reveals a neon scene,
            Hidden from sight.
        Richness, control, and depth,
                              Colored pencils are another way,
                                        Soft and vibrant,
Prismatic feelings   Like plants on display.
            Mixing and blending
Ink or markers, forming   Oils as dancing jellyfish,
In mind, or on paper,   Pigments from soil to sight,
            Capturing emotional light.

The Galloping Guardian

Undoubtedly the best beast,
No one knows its magical feats.
Infinitely loved, graceful dreams,
Celerity, fortitude, and a soft pink.
Over the rainbow it leaps,
Regal blaze, bright and serene,
Never tamed, born to be free.

Prehistoric Corndogs

Think dinosaurs eating corndogs.
Think of the way they eat them all.
The poor T-Rex, with arms not long,
Also trying to eat corndogs,
He is likely to twist and fall.

Is that why all T-Rex are gone?
Did they not eat enough corndogs?
No cheese filled beef, or regular too,
No honey in wheat, sad and so blue.
They can't dip in sweet sauce, yellow or red,
Or even pink if mixed with white instead.

No deliciousness, none at all,
Poor T-Rex, whose arms are too small.

Neko

Crunching in the night,
Agile, air in the soft glow,
Tactile sentiment,
Elegant with style,
Arrow in shadows, docile,
Tonight, full, sleeping.

Sailing For Words

Sunny skies loom above,
 Even clouds have their fun,
  Every breeze guides the sail,
   Soon the storm will avail.

Even clouds have their fun.
 After thoughts know the smell,
  Soon the storm will avail.
   Eager echoes speak none.

After thoughts know the smell,
 Sails change beneath the depth.
  Eager echoes speak none,
   A treasure all have won.

Sails change beneath the depth.
 Every breeze guides the sail.
  A treasure all have won,
   Sunny skies loom above.

A Good Time

A new adventure.
German beer, food, time to talk.
Chocolate mead, too!

Stillness

Chilly Thoughts

Thoughts come and go,   *I always stay.*
Move back and forth,   *sitting fireplace.*
Vacillate in my head,   *sprinkle like soft rain.*
I want sleep instead,   *feeling ever gray.*
Whenever I'm in bed,   *lightning starts to stray.*
Echoes begin to slow,   *eyes rest closing the day.*
The warmth I feel stops,   *chills from outside,*
How my heart melts,   *icy remains weep.*
Once cruel gentle beats,   *creeping cold streaks*
Humming softly beneath,   *glaciers move free,*
Kindness reigns supreme,   *frozen hearts speak.*

Counting Before Sleep

How many do I have to count until I sleep?
1, 2... too many to count, where are the sheep?
When did I lose track? Time or me?
Can't count, combined streams.
How many tears did I count before sleep?

My Lethargy and Empathy

I find it so hard to pick up my pen,
Feeling so heavy, how to begin and when?
The sadness just stops me, then I wonder,
"Where does it end?"
Can't reconcile thoughts once again.
Someone has the feeling inside,
But doesn't have what's in my mind.
I need to fight, just write it this time,
So they can find the help when it's read.

Lost in Waiting

Does dreaming of your face make you stay real,
When I suddenly feel, I need to kneel?
How does time make space to bandage or heal,
When life was torn like shredded orange peels?
No voice to hear, disappear in a day?
Why do you have to go, when I had stayed?
My life was saved but fate couldn't be swayed.
You helped me breathe when oxygen delayed.
So why do I wake up, but nightmares stay?
Learned to let go, but memories remain.
I don't have precious pictures or fun frames.
Seventy years, is afterlife a place?
I guess the story has chapters to gain,
As life moves on, but not yours, I still wait.

Unburdened

Feeling guilty for leaving me behind,
To face the terrors from a fierce fiend.

I faced the terrors as I faced the fiend,
My movements ceased, fear quickly pierced.

Fear quickly pierced, freezing in slow tears.
My heartbeat rings within silence.

Beating thoughts within silence, I grow,
As I remember haunting darkened days.

Darkened days fade, once haunting me,
Until I found courage to be my strength.

My strength born in courage permits,
To forgive as wounds receive a balm.

Forgiveness became my healing balm.
So why feel guilty about leaving me?

Releasing the Past

No future comes,   *as backward steps creak,*
From a present bound,   *to shatter silence,*
Chained with the past,   *hollow spaces grow,*
Regrets held by sorrows,   *mining false gems,*
Anger tearing to shreds,   *foundations of stone,*
Never to lie with smiles,   *as stars never born,*
As memories and pain set,   *the path forward begins,*
Only walls appear,   *crumbling with hope.*

My Persistent Friend

Hello my persistent friend,
I feel your cold embrace,
Time has yet to jog,
Yet you appear unannounced again.

I feel your cold embrace,
Sadness, you shock my heart.
Yet you appear unannounced again,
Always keeping me in the dark.

Sadness, you shock my heart,
Time has yet to jog,
Always keeping me in the dark,
Hello my persistent friend.

Insecure as Silicate

I fight the illusions in my mind,
Where is the twisting peace I seek?
Will the truth, to my soul, unwind?
Remove the pain of ancient streaks.

Where is the twisting peace I seek?
I refuse to hold the fading sand.
Remove the pain of ancient streaks:
Thoughts of doubts strung of lies.

I refuse to hold the fading sand.
Will the truth, to my soul, unwind,
Thoughts of doubts strung of lies?
I fight the illusions in my mind.

Disillusioned

Was this my parent's dream?
Journeying toward freedom, with worn tattered feet.
War creeping into homes, to die or to flee.
Failure is unacceptable, the goal must be seen.

Journeying toward freedom, with worn tattered feet.
The future shines bright, bursting vigor in the spring.
Failure is unacceptable, the goal must be seen.
Without hope, where would they be?

The future shines bright, bursting vigor in the spring.
Stolen by promises, broken, uncouth smokescreen.
Without hope, where would they be?
Struggling to accept the icy sting.

Stolen by promises, broken, uncouth smokescreen
Fear reigning, down with hope and peace.
Struggling to accept the icy sting.
The orange dusk brings shadow from the east

Fear reigning, down with hope and peace.
War creeping into homes, to die or to flee.
The orange dusk brings shadow from the east.
Was this my parent's dream?

Now Is Your Chance

You sought only the fruit,
Though the laborer was hated.
Unkind in your pursuit,
When you should have only waited.

Unpresent for the toil,
As the roots took their first breath.
Failing harvest from soil,
The laborer had no rest.

Your hastiness only brought wroth,
Bitterness to the tree.
Joining mid-season, nothing wrought,
Gratitude it should be.

Inherited when the laborer leaves,
The ground is yours, have the loot.
Plow the fields, plant the seeds, water the trees,
Left to pick your own grown fruit.

Echoes

My Dear Friend

You were there in my darkest times,
It meant a lot to me.
Even if you can't visit,
This doesn't make you any less.

It meant a lot to me.
Even if you're gone,
This doesn't make you any less.
I'm grateful for the memories.

Even if you're gone.
Even if you can't visit,
I'm grateful for the memories.
You were there in my darkest times.

Through the Screen

How do you tell a stranger,
"Come talk to me"?
Strangers, not friends I'd wager,
Just stand, let it be.
How do you say the words that might pry?
Knowing that it causes them to cry?
How do we ask for their pain,
When we can't console? It's the same.
So I'll watch, all in vain.
Through my screen, for it to remain.

Refracted in the Sky

I saw your bright diminishing light,
Fading past rocks, as I start to drive.
The flickering glow, nobody knows,
I saw them all unfold.
Your slow soft glow, many patterns it showed,
Like someone took the volume to low.
The colors of spring, the few in between,
As aurum turned red, fleeing the scene.
Shadows started to creep, inching near me,
The night came, the rainbow now unseen.

The Unclear Night

None hear the beauty in your still silence,
Ocean of lights, small spheres with gaps between,
The two eyes that glare, with a pale faint green.
Hiding behind absorbed photons so near,
Inside fog, even darkness blends unclear.
Narrow strips of red, lining the unknown,
Gone are the ways of hope on roads once shown.
No moonlight, yet there is a soft white gaze,
Ever eternal, misty wisps that fade.
Silvery haze covering that which sways,
Silk screen of beauty, absent of displays.

When I Cry

Pondering, "Does anyone care if I cry?"
All alone. I fear that I will run dry.

I run. Drying my face from their eyes.
No one will see what I hold deep inside.

Cracks reveal deep inside, all of the pain.
Only those who care, will see my disdain.

My disdain toward myself. Clearly it shows.
People couldn't care. This time on my own.

All on my own, I cry for the people.
So they will know that someone else cares.

Someone cares. They know it like I do.
I became what I needed. Only with love.

Only love needed to become what they need.
No more pondering. I care if you cry.

Our Captain, Our Genie

"It is always the happy ones", they say,
"Who bring a smile to your face, too."

To your face, bringing a visage of joy,
Who knows what is hidden underneath?

Underneath, sadness hides within the unknown.
Brought forth freely by those who care.

Freely caring about those brought near,
Spreading love to those held so dear.

Dear love, hold me when I feel spread thin.
Illuminate whenever I feel dim.

I bring light because dim I have been.
They are seen, so they won't disappear.

But I am first to disappear from the world.
"It is always the happy ones," they say.

In My Thoughts

"I care too much", because they can't see,
I cheer and cheer, yet loneliness is near.

Loneliness is near and cheers, I think,
"Do they wonder about me too?", but I doubt.

They wonder and wander without doubt,
Being fruitful in endeavors, filled with glee.

Enduring surprises, I fill with glee,
Grateful for my friends, thriving with ease.

Thriving with ease, friends despite distance,
Sending love, hidden within sacred space.

Within sacred space, expressing I care,
Smiling inside, silence ending here.

Here, smiling inside, never will I say,
"I care too much", because they can't see.

Paused by the Shore

Such wonder fills the air,
As mine slowly leaves.
For a gaze so divine,
Rarely comes to me.
What splendor and beauty,
As salt skips asea.
Azur waves subduing,
Longing for my sleep.
Depths drawing, stars watching,
Mirroring night's peace.
Stretching along brown shores,
Tinted rosy skies.
Slender beams are shining,
See rare pearls ecru.
I stand ashore hoping,
Ocean regards too.

Quiet Reunion

I love that bright-eyed look,
Like stars glazed with honey.   So, why does silence steal
                                  unspoken words?
        A moment of sweetness,

                                  Fog accretes in my mind,
                                  Imploring
                    Listen,   Validation.
                                  The air growing stale
        The rain gently speaks   As the conversation never
                                  starts.

            Growing in volume,
Drips, drops, a slight breeze,   Pursuing peace that pacifies
                                  Inquietude.
        Glad you're here with me.
Precious time takes a seat.   Speaking enough to occupy
        Words with no tasks,
    your gaze center-stage.   Silence.

        Present, in a sea of sugar, and wonder.
          Staring at me, then "I love you"-
            Silence, once heavy, feels light.

Defiance

Kaiju, Inside

Sorry for the monster, *once I used to be,*
Destruction as a pathway, *blocked as I breathe.*
Better not to bother, *pardoning the grievance,*
What else could be done, *weeping for relief.*
Cities are now different, *like moon phases each,*
Razed by the sun, *spirits altering.*
Timing possibly so bad, *learning misfortune for me,*
Misbelief inside the heart, *bringing agony.*
Splintering and shattering, *guilt from the past,*
Tearing thunder apart, *striking lightning fast,*
Piercing the core, *destroying the last,*
As monster ceases to be, *part of who I am.*

Finding My Wings

Light come rescue me, *as I fall into black,*
I gently feel warmth, *I embrace it all.*
Glowing in my soul, *fate bursts small cracks,*
Budding like the earth, *a sea standing tall.*
Give rise to my wings, *slowly I descend,*
Give lift to the sky, *strength from within.*
I beam radiance, *moving like waves,*
When sunshine arrives, *darkness has its end.*

To Go Beyond

We push the boundaries, erasing lines,
Exploring the lands, both low and high.

Both low and high, following river's streams.
We find the falls, where many lose dreams.

Don't lose dreams, forests need a path.
The coast line awaits those who pass tough trees.

Clearing tough trees to fashion wooden boats,
Set forth a-sea, toward the storms unknown.

In storms unknown, we look to the sky,
In wonder, amazed at how birds still fly.

We still fly in wonder, man's limit burst.
Near live stars, but nigh is the earth.

Distant is the earth beneath, what is next?
We push the boundaries, erasing lines.

I Become Not

I can't rewind, *the mistakes- I accept,*
That I'm weak, *bruising my future,*
Feeling fear to, *forswear flickering dreams.*
Give up, *splintering lies of the heart,*
Run not, *from my shadow,*
what reward exists, *quitting before I start?*
I become not, *a husk devoid of feeling,*
If I destroy everything, *burning doubt,*
I can finally stop, *denying my light.*

There's the Door

Why don't you just leave me,
I'm tired of this abuse.
I refuse, you argue, me you use,
It's a ruse, a fickle folly few too.
I choose, you undo, you shrewd,
Bloody words, slashing minds,
Bruising hearts, bashing lives,
You sick scheming scoundrel,
Stop saying such stupid slime.
Why wonder what wild wishes,
Would wear upon my soul?
You're an embarrassment, egomaniacal,
Eagerly etching my defeat,
Don't dare dropping on my dreams,
I'll fight you in my sleep.
I'll fight you in the day, evening and the night,
I'm tired of your lies, leave my lovely light.
You are my doubt, Doubt, I now see,
Self-doubt, insecurity, is all that you bring.
Take it all with you, even the mat if you please,
I'm healing all your trauma, Doubt, let me be.

Freedom to Be

Let me be.
I finally found the words to describe what I seek,
The simple peace.
My identity.
Like the various colors I find in a potted plant.
I seek to find my pieces, so I simply ask, "Let me be."
Whether I feel buried in life, or red inside,
Fuming with anger that I can't hide,
Please, I ask of you, "let it be."
When I ask you to see me for what I see,
And not what I appear to be,
You know, this is a piece of me,
So give me peace.
I change from yellow to green, or others in between,
I might be orange for the season, but next time,
Plucked and unseen,
So please let me be.
I find myself as a seed growing to breathe,
And as I lie peacefully, I want to be seen for me,
I want to be at peace with this piece of me,
So let it be.

Snow, Salt, Sky

White field below my feet, *seeing as if a dream,*
Fading into a lighter blue, *darkened as I go through.*
Split apart by the heat, *brown hidden underneath,*
Droplets form in the day, *giving shade when it's gray.*
Impossible to step on, *leaving earth intact,*
Swirls and peaks match, *figures as salt on a tray.*
Breaking as I watch, *moving as I stay,*
Patterns near the ground, *yet so far away.*

4-3-4

Letting go useless things,
Only keep what you need.
Vengeance won't help you bring
Everything lost between.
Altering minds, you see?
Never leaves, so just breathe.
Don't give what you received.
How do we learn to grieve?
Attacking ourselves, please,
Time to see, their pain bleeds.
Especially, for peace.

Unrecognized Greatness

Being strong isn't being blind,
Seeing wrong isn't turning right.
I try with grace to give my self,
but you can't do it, so "oh well".
I try to obtain all your help,
But you can't, I'll do it myself.

What Lies Beneath

Silent, sharp blades that ever shift.
Hidden hunter, snatch prey unseen.
Ancient of days, strong and tough.
Rough scales, like sand yet latent.
Keen, electric fields unbidden.
Swift fusiform so defiant.

Compassion

I Love Me, Too

I have the rhythm, but
Burning,

You're the beat to my
heart.

The disdain toward myself,

Felt through space and time.

Eating my soul, by slowly,

Echoing my movements,

Rebounding inside,

Mirroring my thoughts.

But I see it now,

A dancing flame,

A power that alters me,

Freezing the darkness.

Finding a way to exist,

By seeing your light,

Seeing that it's the same,

Goodness, and beauty,

I submit,

Compassion grows.

The mirror to my soul,
Helping me behold myself,
Teaching me to love me, too,
Thanks to loving you.

Loved In Different Lights

Real friends, | *let me change when scarlet,*
Outstretched oft, | *knowing I would be rust.*

Young Canary, | *I would be, eager, foolish,*
Giving my jade soul, | *yearning for love.*

But love would rescue, | *my azure soul*
In twilight depths, | *seeing kaleidoscopic shifts.*

Vexing my normal depths, | *soothing lavender calms,*
Viewing the orchids, | *within my troubled heart.*

In midnight trouble, | *accepting transformation,*
Brewing over me, | *like gentle cerulean vines.*

Growing gentle vines, | *without limelight obscuring,*
Yet, remaining by, | *the light lemon joy,*

Overjoyed, grateful, | *reviving coral spirit,*
Real friends, | *let me change when scarlet.*

Heading Home

Moonlight enchants all around,
Such splendor, too bright to recall.
I reflect, wax spirit and mind,
Find peace floating, gentle sky.
Fall nears, ending Summer's touch,
Sound sleeping, bidding goodnight.

Ascending Toward Bliss

Noticed by a woman,
A moment of content.
To receive such a smile,
Pleasing that it was sent.
Hard not to be happy,
Accepting the first date.
Becoming a couple,
So joyful and so great.
But having a daughter,
Where does elation end?
A hero in their eyes,
Ecstatic to defend.
Running into your arms,
Overjoyed not to miss.
The princess full of love,
To have is life's pure bliss.

A Snowflake in Hand

I touched the snow.
An unexpected moment initiated with curiosity.
I beheld the beauty before it came to me.
So I stared.
Thoughts frozen,
Filling the gap with silence.
I held in my hand greatness.
Sublimation,
As the moment fades.
But while with me,
Unearned joy.

The Isle's Gift

"Do you love me?"
Is that actually a thought?
Out of many treasures, is it that I forgot?
Searching inside the fridge,
A miner finding gems.
Opalite white, Garnet red,
Rhodochrosite? Maybe not.
Tourmaline green, whatever is left.
Mixing a concoction of the gems lying around,
Paired with a side of rice this time, and for now.
Working as the dawn moves before it wakes,
Returning when the western sun runs to play.
A stomach empty of the jewels,
Lacking ferrum for the heme,
Weakening each day to have ends meet.
Refusing a plate of goodness,
For the future needs feed,
Lying that there's fullness,
So you'll receive what I don't eat.
Isolated island, giving all your gifts.
Surely they do not go amiss.
Dear mom, my thoughts forgot not.
Love me, you do.

Celebrate Life

When I die, I don't want you to cry,
But I know you will.
I don't want tears wasted on my death,
Rather joy, over the time well spent.
Laugh for the moments you didn't miss,
And miss me for my love unkept.

Our paths crossed once,
Your atramentum stained, etched onto mine,
Seeing past paths, smiling behind.
Raise your head, like you lifted mine,
Rejoice instead, hush those weeping eyes.
I know you weep still, so it shall be,
But live without regrets, I know you loved me.

Waking Spirit

Like a maiden of the forest, *coming from nightfall,*
Clad in mostly green, *shadows drape- a silhouette.*
Gently touching my mind, *oh mistress of raven locks,*
"Awake" your voice booming, *as lightning in my heart.*
Burning hair ever vibrant, *hovering softly with grace,*
Light radiates all about, *extending darkened shades.*
Peacefully guarding, *stillness over all,*
Forests all around, *growing forever bound.*

What A Life

You kindly said "hello" to me,
A cold spring, fields and hills green.

Fields and hills, such is life, growing,
You accepted everything, all of me.

Saying I do, all of me is for you.
Buying homes, parenting, learning how.

Learning how to bloom in love, we change,
Rooms, two to three, beginning anew.

Two to three years, but feeling eternal,
Looking forward to sun tea and books.

So much life to live, looking forward,
To the day we grow to bloom.

Cheers! To the day I fondly remember,
You kindly said "hello" to me.

The Hope That Stayed

"I believe in you."
Those words brought me light.
The stone marks the path.
Darkness at the start.

Those words brought me light.
Reflect across mirrors.
Darkness at the start.
Now a river, running.

Reflect across mirrors.
"Is this truly my life?"
Now a river, running.
Unyielding inside me.

"Is this truly my life?"
The stone marks the path.
Unyielding inside me,
"I believe in you."

Across the Board

I usually feel like a pawn, I am a knight.
You treat me like a king, making me feel alright.
Presence emboldens, unshaken like a rook,
But I am the knight, not easily unhooked.
The most important one is you, my true queen,
You are powerful, coveted, always seen.

I'll gladly dance around the board for you,
Take on the world, Taking a turn or two.
I'm the knight who jumps in front of the fire,
I will take the pawns and the hits so dire.
I'll protect you, my queen, at all times,
Because you chose me, chose to be mine.

You, my love, the kind queen,
courteously divine,
Protecting your heart's king,
Checking to win this fight.

Worth Shaping Or

Will it be enough?
How will I know that it is good?
Is my essence like gold?
Do people rush to find what's deep within my heart?
Bringing pickaxes, water, and wagon or cart,
Rushing to mine, mining with haste,
Digging the dirt as the sun beats on the face.
Will you move your feet,
Stampede as a wave,
Speedily toward me?

This essence, my ichor, drips onto the page,
It holds my sadness, my doubt, my rage.
It is the fiery etherealness coursing my veins,
It too, holds my joy, that I earned through pain.

But the question lingers still,
Will I be enough?
It's rough, like a blast of desert air,
Scraping my thoughts smooth and fair.
But I love it.
So it's gold to me.
It's my metal made into a leaf.

Dream

Believe, stars shine free.
Courage, strength to chase the heart.
Dreams, finally yours.

Appendix

Poetry Forms

The following forms appear throughout this collection. Their names are not listed in the titles, allowing readers to discover their presence organically.

Acrostic
Acrostic poetry has roots tied to ancient Greek and Latin traditions. The poems arrange the first letters of each line to spell out a word or phrase vertically—often the subject or theme of the poem. While typically written in free verse, the form can vary in complexity.

Bella
Bella poetry was created by Alemseged Sisay in Addis Ababa, Ethiopia. The form consists of six lines with a mirrored rhyme pattern between opening and closing words.

Cleave
Cleave poetry was created by Dr. Phuoc-Tan Diep in 2006. The form consists of two vertical poems—left and right columns—that can be read independently, as well as a third poem formed by reading across both columns line by line.

Contrapuntal

Contrapuntal poetry draws its name from contrapunto, the Italian word for "counterpoint." Two or more poems are placed side by side—often in columns—and can be read vertically, horizontally, or as a unified third voice. The origin is unclear, but Russian poet Andrei Bely used contrapuntal techniques in 1921. The form gained attention in the 21st century through poets like Tyehimba Jess, Tarfia Faizullah, and Brian Bilston.

Duplex

Duplex poetry was created by Jericho Brown in 2019. The form blends elements of the sonnet, ghazal, and blues poem into a sequence of seven couplets. Each second line is echoed in the first line of the next couplet, and the final line repeats the first.

Free Verse

Free verse poetry became prominent in the 19th century. It is a form that does not follow a fixed meter, rhyme scheme, or structure. Instead, it flows with the natural rhythms of speech, allowing the poet full creative freedom.

Haiku

Haiku is a traditional Japanese poetic form from the 17th century. The form consists of three lines with a 5-7-5 rhythm. In Japanese, this pattern is measured in morae —sound units more precise than syllables, accounting for long vowels and consonants. While English haiku often mimic this 5-7-5 structure using syllables, the original rhythm and pacing are deeply rooted in the Japanese language.

Pantoum

Pantoum poetry originated in 15th-century Malaysia and is composed of four-line stanzas with a unique pattern of repetition. The second and fourth lines of each stanza become the first and third lines of the next. The final stanza typically circles back to the opening, completing the poem's cyclical form.

Pentameter

Pentameter is rooted in Greek and Latin prosody. It refers to a line of poetry composed of five metrical feet. While often associated with iambic patterns, the term itself does not require a specific rhythm. Lines typically contain around ten syllables, offering a steady and versatile cadence used in both traditional and contemporary verse.